MILITARY AIRCRAFT

F-35
LIGHTNING II

BY DONNA MCKINNEY

TORQUE™

BELLWETHER MEDIA • MINNEAPOLIS, MN

Torque brims with excitement perfect for thrill-seekers of all kinds. Discover daring survival skills, explore uncharted worlds, and marvel at mighty engines and extreme sports. In *Torque* books, anything can happen. Are you ready?

This edition first published in 2024 by Bellwether Media, Inc.

No part of this publication may be reproduced in whole or in part without written permission of the publisher. For information regarding permission, write to Bellwether Media, Inc., Attention: Permissions Department, 6012 Blue Circle Drive, Minnetonka, MN 55343.

Library of Congress Cataloging-in-Publication Data

Names: McKinney, Donna B. (Donna Bowen), author.
Title: F-35 Lightning II / by Donna McKinney.
Description: Minneapolis, MN : Bellwether Media, Inc., 2024. | Series: Torque: Military Aircraft | Includes bibliographical references and index. | Audience: Ages 7-12 | Audience: Grades 4-6 | Summary: "Engaging images accompany information about the F-35 Lightning II. The combination of high-interest subject matter and light text is intended for students in grades 3 through 7"– Provided by publisher.
Identifiers: LCCN 2023046765 (print) | LCCN 2023046766 (ebook) | ISBN 9798886878202 (library binding) | ISBN 9798886879148 (ebook)
Subjects: LCSH: F-35 (Military aircraft)–Juvenile literature. | Fighter planes–United States.
Classification: LCC UG1242.F5 M3235 2024 (print) | LCC UG1242.F5 (ebook) | DDC 623.74/63-dc23/eng/20231006
LC record available at https://lccn.loc.gov/2023046765
LC ebook record available at https://lccn.loc.gov/2023046766

Text copyright © 2024 by Bellwether Media, Inc. TORQUE and associated logos are trademarks and/or registered trademarks of Bellwether Media, Inc.

Editor: Kieran Downs   Designer: Jeffrey Kollock

Printed in the United States of America, North Mankato, MN.

TABLE OF CONTENTS

SEEING THE BATTLEFIELD	4
WHAT IS THE F-35 LIGHTNING II?	6
ONE AIRCRAFT, MANY USES	10
BUILDING FOR THE FUTURE	18
F-35 LIGHTNING II FACTS	20
GLOSSARY	22
TO LEARN MORE	23
INDEX	24

SEEING THE BATTLEFIELD

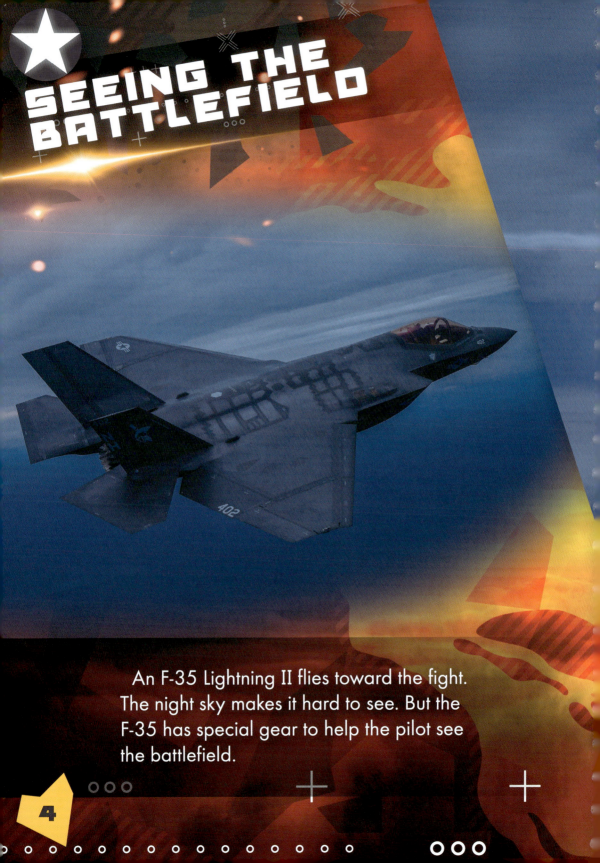

An F-35 Lightning II flies toward the fight. The night sky makes it hard to see. But the F-35 has special gear to help the pilot see the battlefield.

4

The plane's technology lets the pilot know where the enemy is hiding. The pilot finds the target. The F-35 opens fire and destroys it!

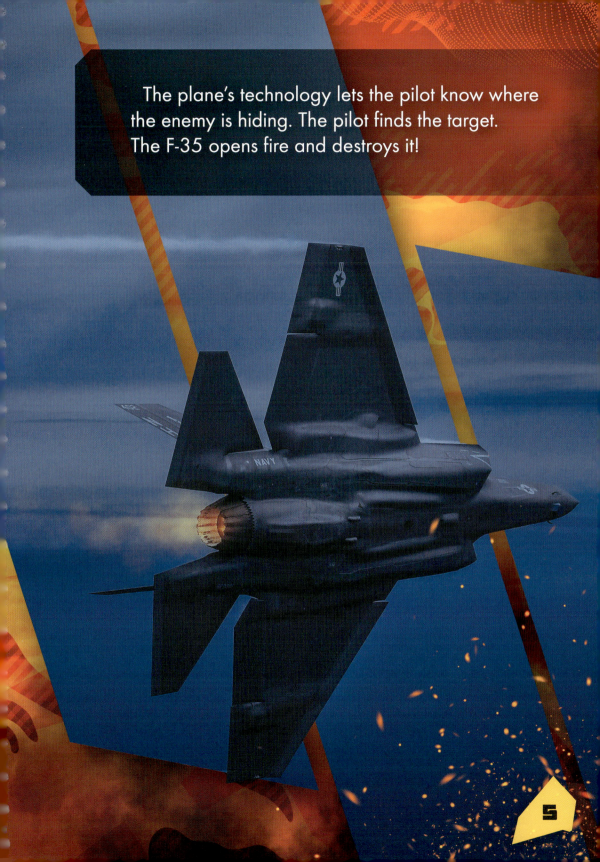

WHAT IS THE F-35 LIGHTNING II?

The F-35 Lightning II is a fighter jet. The first F-35s were built in 2006.

There are three F-35 aircraft. The F-35A is built for the United States Air Force. The F-35B is built for the U.S. Marine Corps. The F-35C is built for the U.S. Navy and Marine Corps. The main difference between the aircraft is the way they take off and land.

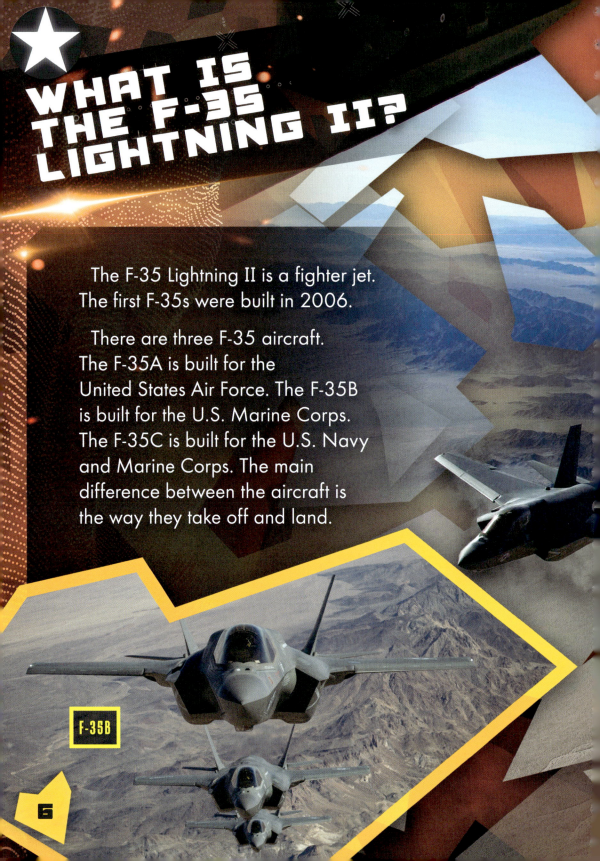

F-35B

THE PLANE'S NAME

The F-35 Lightning II is named after the P-38 Lightning. The P-38 was used in World War II.

F-35C

The F-35 was built to replace the F-16, A-10, F/A-18, and AV-8B aircraft. The F-35B flew its first **combat** missions in Afghanistan in 2018.

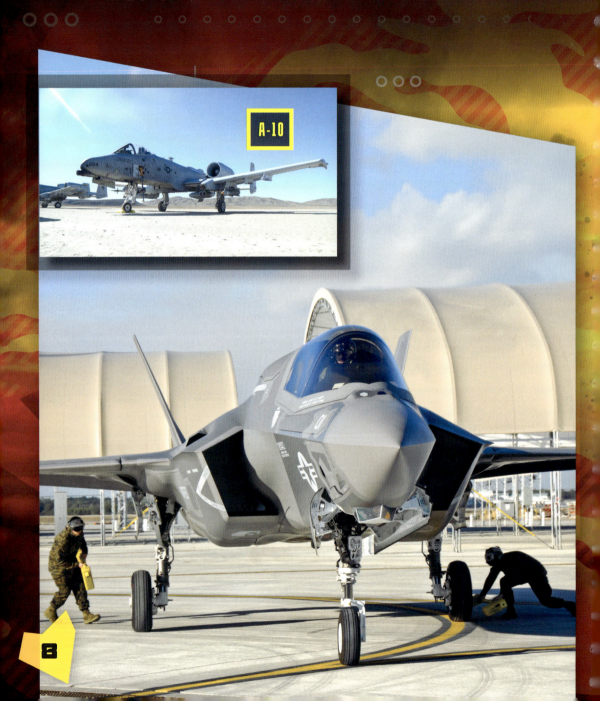

A-10

The F-35A flew its first combat missions in Iraq in 2019. Starting in 2022, F-35s were used to help Ukraine in their fight against Russia.

F-35A

MISSIONS MAP

Supporting Ukraine in the fight against Russia
Ukraine, 2022

Fighting against Islamic State of Iraq and Syria (ISIS)
Iraq, 2019

Fighting against Taliban
Afghanistan, 2018

ONE AIRCRAFT, MANY USES

In 1995, the military wanted to replace many kinds of aircraft. They decided to use one plane to replace all of them. It needed to be fast and **stealthy**. It also needed to be used in battle by many **branches** of the military.

10

SIZE CHART

LENGTH
51 FEET (15.5 METERS)

HEIGHT
14 FEET (4.3 METERS)

WIDTH AND WINGSPAN
35 FEET (10.7 METERS)

Test flights of the F-35 began in 2000. It was first used by the Air Force in 2011.

The F-35 fights enemies in the air and on the ground. It carries **missiles** and bombs. It also carries a **cannon**. The cannon can fire 3,000 rounds per minute.

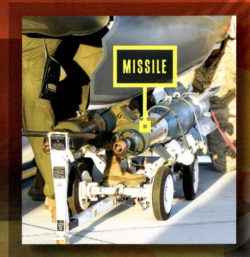

PARTS OF AN F-35B LIGHTNING II

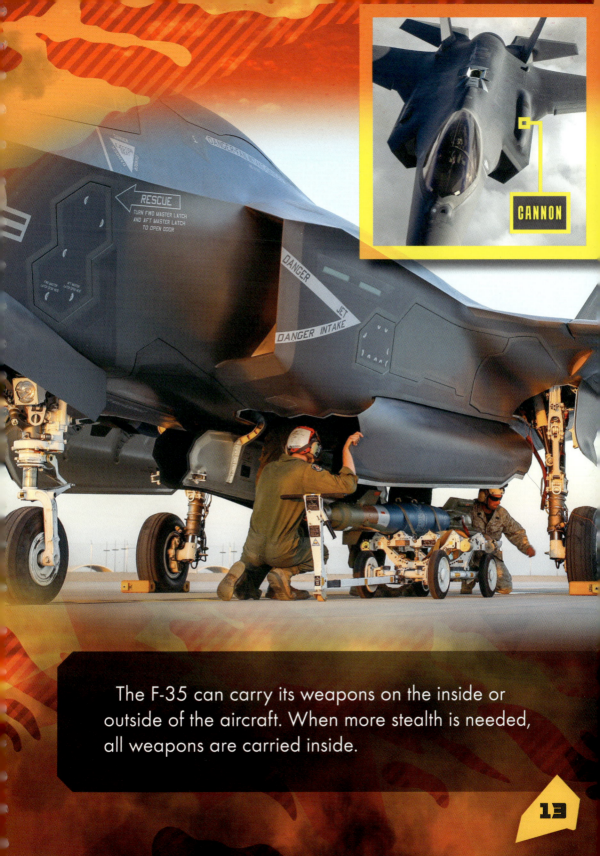

CANNON

The F-35 can carry its weapons on the inside or outside of the aircraft. When more stealth is needed, all weapons are carried inside.

The F-35 crew is one pilot. The pilot's helmet displays information. It helps the pilot see the enemy and find targets easier and faster. The **cockpit** also has a display. It gives the pilot helpful information.

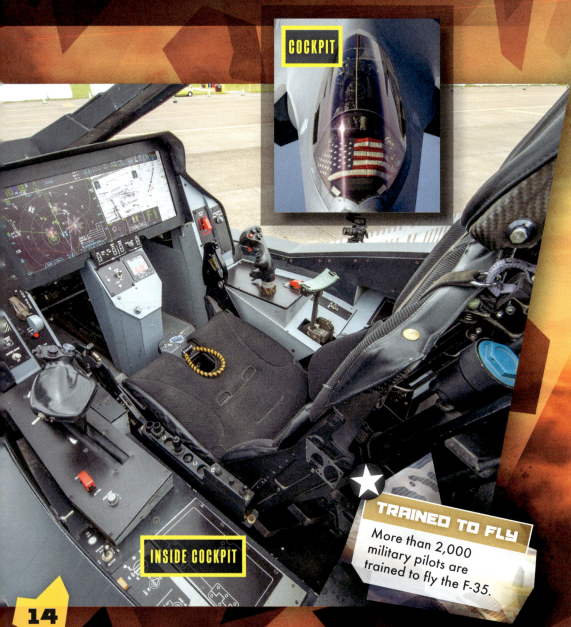

COCKPIT

INSIDE COCKPIT

TRAINED TO FLY
More than 2,000 military pilots are trained to fly the F-35.

F-35 PILOT'S HELMET

NIGHT VISION

MOUNTED DISPLAY SYSTEM

360 DEGREE VIEW CAMERAS

SENSOR

Sensors can show the pilot the enemy's location. The F-35 is also loaded with powerful computers. They help it **communicate** with other aircraft and ground **forces**.

15

The F-35's stealth features hide it from enemies.
It can see the enemy long before the enemy sees it.
The body of the F-35 is covered in a coating.
This helps it hide from **radar**. Its shape also helps it hide.

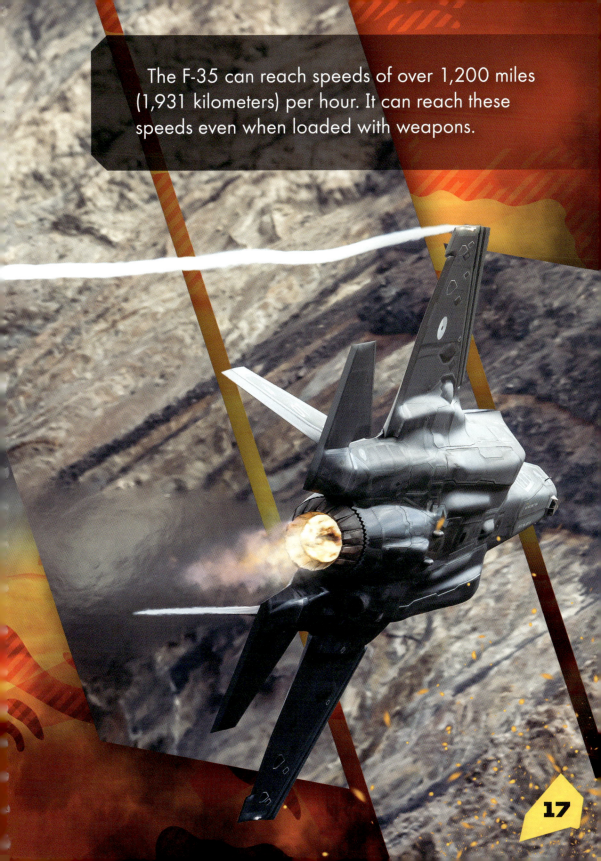

The F-35 can reach speeds of over 1,200 miles (1,931 kilometers) per hour. It can reach these speeds even when loaded with weapons.

BUILDING FOR THE FUTURE

The F-35's technology continues to improve. The newest F-35s will have more powerful computers. They will have better displays in the cockpit.

The U.S. military plans to keep making F-35s. They plan to keep flying F-35s until 2070. The F-35 will continue to be used around the world for years to come!

F-35 LIGHTNING II FACTS

STATS

TOP SPEED

1,228 miles
(1,976 kilometers)
per hour

RANGE

more than
1,381 miles
(2,222 kilometers)

ALTITUDE CEILING

above 50,000 feet
(15,240 meters)

20

WEAPONS

- **2** AIR-TO-AIR MISSILES
- **2** GUIDED BOMBS
- UP TO **220** ROUNDS

CLASS
5TH GENERATION FIGHTER

CREW
1

OPERATION

MORE THAN **975** F-35 LIGHTNING IIs IN USE TODAY

MANUFACTURER

Lockheed Martin

BRANCHES OF THE MILITARY

U.S. Air Force

U.S. Marine Corps

U.S. Navy

MAIN PURPOSE

stealth multi-role fighter

FIRST YEAR USED

2006

GLOSSARY

branches—divisions of the U.S. military; the branches of the military are the Air Force, Army, Coast Guard, Marines, Navy, and Space Force.

cannon—a large gun

cockpit—the part of an aircraft where the crew sits

combat—related to a fight between armed forces

communicate—to share information with others

forces—military groups

missiles—explosives that are sent to targets

radar—a device that uses energy waves to sense and see objects

sensors—devices that detect objects and send that information to a computer

stealthy—able to be hidden; a stealth aircraft cannot be located by radar.

TO LEARN MORE

AT THE LIBRARY

Colson, Rob. *Awesome Aircraft*. New York, N.Y.: Enslow Publishing, 2023.

Hamilton, John. *United States Air Force*. Minneapolis, Minn.: Abdo Publishing, 2021.

Schuh, Mari. *Military Aircraft*. North Mankato, Minn.: Pebble, 2022.

ON THE WEB

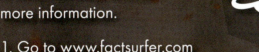

Factsurfer.com gives you a safe, fun way to find more information.

1. Go to www.factsurfer.com

2. Enter "F-35 Lightning II" into the search box and click 🔍.

3. Select your book cover to see a list of related content.

INDEX

A-10, 8
Afghanistan, 8
AV-8B, 8
bombs, 12
branches, 6, 10, 11
cannon, 12, 13
coating, 16
cockpit, 14, 18
combat, 8
computers, 15, 18
display, 14, 18
enemies, 5, 12, 14, 15, 16
F-16, 8
F-35 Lightning II facts, 20–21
F/A-18, 8
forces, 15
future, 18
helmet, 14, 15
history, 6, 7, 8, 9, 10, 11
Iraq, 9
map, 9
missiles, 12
missions, 8, 9
name, 7
P-38 Lightning, 7
parts of an F-35B Lightning II, 12
pilot, 4, 5, 14, 15
radar, 16
Russia, 9
sensors, 15
shape, 16
size, 11
speeds, 10, 17
stealth, 10, 13, 16
types, 6, 7, 8, 9, 12
Ukraine, 9
United States Air Force, 6, 11
United States Marine Corps, 6
United States Navy, 6
weapons, 12, 13, 17

The images in this book are reproduced through the courtesy of: Duncan Bevan/ DVIDS, cover; Tylir Meyer/ DVIDS, p. 3; Shannon Renfoe/DVIDS, pp. 4, 5; Aditya0635, pp. 6, 12 (top, bottom), 13 (cannon), 18, 20 ,23; Leilani Cervantes/ DVIDS, p. 7; Nathan Franco/ DVIDS, p. 8 (A-10); Samuel King Jr./ DVIDS, p. 8; Christine Groening/ DVIDS, p. 9; ranchorunner, p. 10 (fun fact); Tim Laurence/ Wikimedia Commons, p. 10; Artur Shvartsberg/ DVIDS, pp. 12 (missile), 13; Malcolm Park editorial/ Alamy, p. 14; Yosselin Campos/ DVIDS, p. 14 (cockpit); USMC employee/ Wikimedia Commons, p. 15; Juan Martinez/ Wikimedia Commons, p. 15 (sensor); Maciej Kopaniecki, p. 16; Jan Dijkstra/ Wikimedia Commons, p. 17; Ronald Bradshaw/ Wikimedia Commons, p. 19.